RISING ABOVE

OVERCOMING SELF-DOUBT AND DISCOVERING YOUR INNER STRENGTH

ABHISHEK BACHHAV

Made with ♥ on the Notion Press Platform
www.notionpress.com

I would like to dedicate this book to two incredible sources of knowledge and inspiration - ChatGPT and Google.

To ChatGPT - your vast knowledge and insightful responses have been an invaluable resource throughout the writing of this book. You have helped me to explore and learn about a wide range of topics, and your tireless efforts to provide the best possible answers have been truly remarkable.

To Google - your ability to search through countless pages of information in an instant has been nothing short of amazing. You have helped me to expand my research beyond what I thought was possible, and your wealth of resources have been essential to the development of this book.

Thank you, ChatGPT and Google, for your unwavering commitment to knowledge and learning. Your dedication to helping people discover and explore new ideas has been an essential part of my writing journey, and I am grateful for all that you have done.

Sincerely,

Abhishek Bachhav

Contents

Preface

This book is the result of countless questions I asked to ChatGPT and Google about the topic of rising above self-doubt. I have taken this information and restructured it into a comprehensive book that covers the most essential aspects of overcoming self-doubt.

We all face self-doubt at some point in our lives. It can be a crippling feeling that holds us back from achieving our goals and reaching our full potential. But what if I told you that rising above self-doubt is possible? That there are ways to break free from its grasp and live a life of confidence and purpose?

In writing this book, I wanted to explore this topic in-depth, and I turned to two incredible sources of knowledge and inspiration - ChatGPT and Google. I asked them countless questions about self-doubt, confidence, and self-esteem, and I was amazed at the wealth of information they provided.

I have taken this information and restructured it into easy-to-digest chapters that cover the most important aspects of rising above self-doubt. Each chapter is designed to provide practical tips and strategies that you can use to overcome self-doubt and build confidence.

In the following pages, you'll learn how to identify and address the root causes of self-doubt, how to develop a growth mindset, and how to build self-esteem through self-compassion and self-care. You'll also find tools and exercises that you can use to reframe negative self-talk, overcome imposter syndrome, and take action towards your goals.

I hope this book will be a valuable resource for anyone who struggles with self-doubt and wants to build confidence and self-belief. By the end of this book, I believe you'll have the knowledge, skills, and motivation you need to rise above self-doubt and achieve your full potential.

CHAPTER ONE

UNDERSTANDING SELF-DOUBT

A. Definition and Causes of Self-Doubt

Self-doubt is a complex phenomenon that can stem from a variety of factors. At its core, self-doubt is a state of uncertainty or lack of confidence in oneself and one's abilities. People who experience self-doubt may doubt their own worth, competence, or effectiveness in a particular area.

One common cause of self-doubt is past experiences. If someone has experienced failure, rejection, or negative feedback in the past, they may be more likely to doubt themselves in the future. For example, if someone was criticized harshly for a mistake they made at work, they may begin to doubt their ability to do their job effectively. Similarly, if someone failed to achieve a goal they set for themselves, they may doubt their ability to succeed in that area in the future.

Another cause of self-doubt is negative self-talk. Negative self-talk is the internal dialogue that individuals have with themselves, often without even realizing it. This internal dialogue can be critical, judgmental, and self-defeating. Negative self-talk can take many forms, such as self-criticism, self-doubt, or self-blame. When someone engages in negative self-talk, they reinforce their self-doubt and make it more challenging to overcome.

Social conditioning is another significant contributor to self-doubt. For example, if someone grows up in an environment where they receive a lot of criticism or are told that they aren't good enough, they may develop self-doubt as a result. Similarly, if someone is socialized to believe that certain groups are superior to others, they may experience self-doubt if they do not fit into those groups. In some cases, social conditioning can lead to internalized beliefs about one's abilities, worth, or value.

Perfectionism is another common cause of self-doubt. When someone sets impossibly high standards for themselves, they may be more likely to doubt their abilities to meet those standards. For example, if someone sets a goal of never making a mistake, they are setting themselves up for failure. When they inevitably make a mistake, they may feel like a failure and doubt their abilities.

Finally, fear of failure can also contribute to self-doubt. When someone is afraid of failing, they may doubt their abilities to succeed. This fear can be paralyzing, making it difficult to take risks or try new thingssome cases, fear of failure can lead to avoidance behaviors, such as procrastination or hesitancy.

In conclusion, self-doubt is a complex phenomenon that can stem from a variety of factors. Past experiences, negative self-talk, social conditioning, perfectionism, and fear of failure are all common causes of self-doubt. By understanding the causes of self-doubt, individuals can begin to recognize and address their own self-doubt, paving the way for a more confident and fulfilling life.

B. How self-doubt manifests in thoughts, feelings, and behaviors

Self-doubt can manifest in a variety of ways, impacting a person's thoughts, feelings, and behaviors. It can lead to negative self-talk, a lack of confidence, and avoidance behaviors. The following are some ways in which self-doubt can manifest:

Negative self-talk: Self-doubt often leads to negative self-talk, which can be critical and judgmental. People who experience self-doubt may tell themselves that they're not good enough or that they'll never succeed. This negative self-talk can make it difficult to move forward and accomplish goals.

Perfectionism: Self-doubt can often lead to perfectionism. People who doubt themselves may set impossibly high standards and become obsessed with avoiding mistakes or failures. This can lead to procrastination or avoidance behaviors, as well as anxiety and stress.

Lack of confidence: Self-doubt can also lead to a lack of confidence. When someone doubts their abilities, they may feel uncertain or insecure, which can impact their confidence levels. This lack of confidence can prevent them from taking risks or trying new things.

Avoidance behaviors: Self-doubt can also lead to avoidance behaviors. When someone doubts their abilities, they may avoid situations or tasks that they perceive as challenging or difficult. This can lead to missed opportunities, as well as feelings of frustration and regret.

Anxiety and stress: Self-doubt can cause anxiety and stress, which can impact a person's mental and physical health. People who doubt themselves may worry excessively about the future, leading to feelings of anxiety and stress.

Negative impact on relationships: Self-doubt can impact relationships with others. People who doubt themselves may become defensive or withdrawn, making it difficult to form connections with others. This can lead to feelings of loneliness and isolation.

Impact on personal development: Self-doubt can also impact personal development. When someone doubts themselves, they may be less likely to pursue their goals and dreams. This can prevent them from reaching their full potential and living a fulfilling life.

In conclusion, self-doubt can manifest in a variety of ways, impacting a person's thoughts, feelings, and behaviors. Negative self-talk, perfectionism, a lack of confidence, avoidance behaviors, anxiety and stress, a negative impact on relationships, and an impact on personal development are all common manifestations of self-doubt. Recognizing these manifestations and working to address them can help individuals overcome their self-doubt and lead a more confident and fulfilling life.

C. Impact of Self-Doubt on Mental Health, Relationships, and Personal Development

Self-doubt can have a significant impact on a person's mental health, relationships, and personal development. The negative effects of self-doubt can be especially harmful when it is chronic or severe. Here are some ways in which self-doubt can impact mental health, relationships, and personal development:

Mental health: Self-doubt can have a profound impact on mental health. It can lead to anxiety, depression, and low self-esteem. When someone doubts their abilities, they may worry excessively about the future, leading to feelings of anxiety and stress. They may also feel hopeless and discouraged, leading to feelings of depression. The negative self-talk associated with self-doubt can also impact self-esteem, leading to a negative view of oneself.

Relationships: Self-doubt can also impact relationships with others. People who doubt themselves may become defensive or withdrawn, making it difficult to form connections with others. They may also be more likely to experience conflict in their relationships, as they may be more sensitive to criticism or rejection. This can lead to feelings of loneliness and isolation, which can further exacerbate self-doubt.

Personal development: Self-doubt can also impact personal development. When someone doubts themselves, they may be less likely to pursue their goals and dreams. This can prevent them from reaching their full potential and living a fulfilling life. The lack of confidence associated with self-doubt can also prevent individuals from taking risks or trying new things, limiting their personal growth and development.

It is important to note that the impact of self-doubt can be cyclical. Self-doubt can lead to negative thoughts and behaviors, which can further reinforce self-doubt. For example, someone who doubts their abilities may avoid challenging situations or tasks, which can prevent them from gaining new experiences or developing new skills. This lack of experience or skill development can further reinforce their self-doubt, leading to a cycle of negative thoughts and behaviors.

However, it is possible to break this cycle and overcome self-doubt. It is important to recognize the impact of self-doubt on mental health, relationships, and personal development and take steps to address it. This can include challenging negative self-talk, setting realistic goals and expectations, seeking support from others, and practicing self-compassion. Seeking

Professional help from a therapist or counselor can also be helpful in addressing self-doubt and its impact on mental health, relationships, and personal development.

In conclusion, self-doubt can have a significant impact on a person's mental health, relationships, and personal development. It can lead to anxiety, depression, low self-esteem, conflict in relationships, and a lack of personal growth and development. Recognizing the impact of self-doubt and taking steps to address it can help individuals overcome their self-doubt and lead a more confident and fulfilling life.

CHAPTER TWO

Identifying and Challenging Negative Self-Talk

A. Recognizing Negative Self-Talk

Negative self-talk is a common experience for many people, but it can be difficult to recognize. It is important to be aware of negative self-talk because it can impact how we feel about ourselves and how we approach challenges. The following are some tips to help recognize negative self-talk:

Pay attention to your thoughts. The first step in recognizing negative self-talk is to become aware of the thoughts that you have throughout the day. Notice any thoughts that are self-critical, self-blaming, or self-doubting. It can be helpful to write down your thoughts in a journal so that you can review them later.

Look for patterns. As you review your thoughts, look for patterns or themes. Do you tend to focus on your weaknesses or failures? Do you have a tendency to catastrophize or overgeneralize? Identifying patterns can help you become more aware of when you are engaging in negative self-talk.

Use mindfulness techniques. Mindfulness involves being present and aware of your thoughts and emotions without judgment. Practicing mindfulness can help you become more aware of negative self-talk and can help you develop a more compassionate and accepting attitude toward yourself.

Get feedback from others. Sometimes it can be difficult to recognize negative self-talk on your own. Asking a trusted friend or therapist for feedback can help you gain insight into your thought patterns.

Identify triggers. Certain situations or people may trigger negative self-talk. Identifying these triggers can help you prepare for them and develop strategies to cope with them.

It is important to remember that negative self-talk is a common experience and that everyone engages in it at times. The goal is not to eliminate negative self-talk entirely, but to recognize it and learn to challenge it in a more constructive way.

B. The Impact of Negative Self-Talk on Self-Esteem and Self-Confidence

Negative self-talk can have a profound impact on an individual's self-esteem and self-confidence. When individuals engage in negative self-talk, they are essentially reinforcing negative beliefs about themselves. This can lead to a downward spiral where individuals begin to believe that they are not capable or worthy, which can further reinforce negative self-talk.

One of the ways that negative self-talk impacts self-esteem is by creating a negative self-image. When individuals engage in negative self-talk, they may focus on their perceived flaws and shortcomings, rather than their strengths and positive attributes. This can lead to a distorted view of oneself, where individuals only see their weaknesses and feel inadequate in various areas of their lives. This can have a profound impact on self-esteem, leading to feelings of worthlessness, low self-confidence, and self-doubt.

Similarly, negative self-talk can impact an individual's self-confidence by undermining their belief in their abilities. When individuals engage in negative self-talk, they may begin to doubt their competence and ability to perform certain tasks. This can lead to a reluctance to take on new challenges or try new things, which can limit their growth and development. Over time, this can erode an individual's self-confidence and lead to a lack of motivation and ambition.

It is important to recognize the impact of negative self-talk on self-esteem and self-confidence and take steps to challenge it. One way to challenge negative self-talk is to replace negative thoughts with positive ones. For example, instead of saying, "I can't do this," individuals can reframe their thoughts and say, "I may struggle with this, but I am capable of learning and growing." This can help to shift the focus from perceived limitations to opportunities for growth and development.

Another technique for challenging negative self-talk is to practice self-compassion. When individuals are kind and understanding towards themselves, they can develop a more positive self-image and build self-esteem. This involves treating oneself with the same kindness and compassion that one would offer to a friend or loved one, rather than engaging in self-criticism and negative self-talk.

Lastly, seeking support from friends, family, or professionals can also be beneficial for challenging negative self-talk. Talking to others can provide perspective and help individuals to reframe their negative thoughts in a more positive light.

In conclusion, negative self-talk can have a significant impact on an individual's self-esteem and self-confidence. However, by recognizing the impact of negative self-talk and taking steps to challenge it, individuals can improve their self-image, build self-esteem, and increase their self-confidence. This can lead to a more positive and fulfilling life, where individuals are able to pursue their goals and aspirations with greater confidence and self-assurance.

C. Techniques to Challenge Negative Self-Talk and Replace it with More Positive Self-Talk

Negative self-talk is a common occurrence that can impact an individual's mental health and overall wellbeing. Challenging negative self-talk is an important step towards developing a more positive self-image, building self-esteem, and increasing self-confidence. Here are some techniques that can be used to challenge negative self-talk and replace it with more positive self-talk:

Identify the negative self-talk: The first step towards challenging negative self-talk is to identify it. This means paying attention to the internal dialogue and recognizing when negative self-talk is occurring. When negative self-talk is identified, individuals can begin to challenge it and replace it with more positive self-talk.

Question the negative self-talk: Once negative self-talk is identified, the next step is to question it. This means asking yourself if the thought is accurate and if there is evidence to support it. Often, negative self-talk is based on irrational or unfounded beliefs, so questioning it can help to reduce its impact.

Reframe the negative self-talk: Reframing negative self-talk involves replacing negative thoughts with more positive ones. This means looking for evidence that contradicts negative beliefs and focusing on more positive aspects of oneself. For example, instead of saying, "I am not good enough," individuals can reframe their thoughts and say, "I have many strengths and abilities that make me a valuable person."

Use positive affirmations: Positive affirmations are statements that are used to reinforce positive beliefs about oneself. These can be repeated as a daily practice to help build self-confidence and self-esteem. For example, individuals can say, "I am capable and confident in all that I do," or "I am worthy and deserving of love and respect."

Practice self-compassion: Self-compassion involves treating oneself with kindness and understanding, rather than criticism and judgment. This means acknowledging and accepting one's flaws and imperfections, while still recognizing one's value and worth. By practicing self-compassion, individuals can develop a more positive self-image and build self-esteem.

Seek support: Seeking support from friends, family, or professionals can be helpful in challenging negative self-talk. Talking to others can provide perspective and help individuals to reframe their negative thoughts in a more positive light. Additionally, working with a therapist can provide tools and techniques for challenging negative self-talk and developing more positive self-talk.

In conclusion, challenging negative self-talk is an important step towards building a more positive self-image and increasing self-confidence. By identifying, questioning, and reframing negative self-talk, using positive affirmations, practicing self-compassion, and seeking support, individuals can develop a more positive and fulfilling life. With these techniques, individuals can learn to cultivate a more positive internal dialogue, which can lead to greater self-esteem, self-confidence, and overall well being.

CHAPTER THREE

Building Self-Confidence

A. Benefits of self-confidence

Self-confidence is a key aspect of a person's personality, which plays a vital role in personal and professional success. It is the belief in one's abilities, qualities, and judgments that allows individuals to take risks, pursue their goals, and overcome obstacles. Here are some benefits of self-confidence:

Increased Resilience: Self-confidence helps individuals to cope with the challenges of life. When a person is confident, they can bounce back from setbacks, failures, and disappointments more easily. Self-confident individuals are more likely to take risks and persevere even when they face obstacles.

Greater Sense of Accomplishment: Confidence in one's abilities allows individuals to tackle new challenges and achieve their goals. When a person is self-confident, they are more likely to set ambitious goals and work towards them with determination. When they accomplish their goals, it increases their sense of accomplishment and satisfaction.

Improved Relationships: Self-confidence can improve the quality of an individual's relationships. When a person is confident, they are more likely to express themselves authentically and assertively, and communicate their needs and boundaries clearly. This can help to build stronger, more honest relationships based on trust and mutual respect.

Increased Career Success: Self-confidence is a critical component of career success. Individuals who are self-confident are more likely to seek out new opportunities, take on leadership roles, and negotiate effectively for promotions and higher salaries. Self-confidence can also help individuals to be more effective communicators, make more strategic decisions, and build strong professional networks.

Improved Mental Health: Self-confidence is an important factor in mental health and well-being. Low self-esteem and self-doubt are often linked to anxiety, depression, and other mental health issues. On the other hand, individuals with high self-confidence tend to have better self-esteem, better coping skills, and lower levels of stress and anxiety.

In conclusion, self-confidence plays an essential role in personal and professional success. Individuals who are confident in their abilities and value are more likely to achieve their goals, build strong relationships, and thrive in their careers. By building self-confidence, individuals can improve their resilience, sense of accomplishment, relationships, career success, and overall mental health and well-being.

B. Practical exercises and techniques to build self-confidence, such as affirmations, visualization, and goal setting

Building self-confidence is a process that requires consistent effort and practice. Here are some practical exercises and techniques that can help individuals build self-confidence:

Affirmations: Affirmations are positive statements that individuals repeat to themselves to reinforce positive beliefs and attitudes. Affirmations can be used to counteract negative self-talk and build a more positive and confident mindset. Some examples of affirmations that can help build self-confidence include: "I am worthy of success," "I am capable of achieving my goals," and "I believe in myself and my abilities."

To make affirmations more effective, it's important to use them consistently and regularly. This can be done by writing them down and reciting them daily, or by using affirmations as a daily meditation or visualization practice.

Visualization: Visualization is a technique that involves creating mental images of oneself succeeding in a particular situation or achieving a specific goal. Visualization can help individuals build self-confidence by allowing them to see themselves as successful and capable. Visualization can be used to prepare for a challenging situation, such as a job interview or public speaking engagement.

To use visualization effectively, individuals should create a clear and vivid mental image of themselves succeeding in the situation. They should focus on the positive feelings and emotions associated with success, such as confidence, competence, and achievement.

Goal Setting: Setting achievable goals can help individuals build self-confidence by providing a sense of accomplishment and progress. It's important to set goals that are specific, measurable, and realistic. For example, if an individual is working to build their self-confidence in a particular area, they could set a goal to take on a small challenge in that area, such as speaking up in a meeting or initiating a conversation with a stranger.

To use goal setting effectively, individuals should break down their larger goals into smaller, manageable steps. This can help them make progress towards their goals and build momentum over time.

Real-life example: Let's say an individual is struggling with self-confidence in their job search. They could use a combination of the above techniques to improve their confidence. For example:

Affirmations: They could create and repeat positive affirmations such as "I am qualified for this job" or "I am confident in my abilities."

Visualization: They could visualize themselves facing a job interview and receiving an offer for their dream job. By focusing on the positive feelings associated with success, they can build their confidence and reduce their anxiety.

Goal Setting: They could set specific and achievable goals, such as submitting three job applications per week or networking with one new contact per week. By achieving these smaller goals, they can build momentum and feel more confident in their job search.

By using these practical exercises and techniques consistently, individuals can build their self-confidence and achieve their goals. It's important to remember that building self-confidence is a process that takes time and effort, but with consistent practice, anyone can develop a more positive and confident mindset.

C. Overcoming obstacles to building self-confidence

Building self-confidence is not an easy process, and it can be hindered by various obstacles. Identifying and addressing these obstacles can help individuals overcome them and continue on their journey towards building self-confidence.

Fear of failure: One of the most common obstacles to building self-confidence is the fear of failure. Fear of failure can make individuals hesitant to take risks or try new things, leading to a lack of growth and development. To overcome this obstacle, individuals need to recognize that failure is a natural part of the learning process, and that every failure is an opportunity for growth and improvement. By reframing their perspective on failure, individuals can shift their focus from avoiding failure to embracing it as an essential step towards success.

Negative self-talk: Negative self-talk can be a significant obstacle to building self-confidence, as it can reinforce feelings of self-doubt and insecurity. Identifying and challenging negative self-talk is crucial for individuals looking to build self-confidence. By replacing negative self-talk with positive affirmations and messages, individuals can change the way they think and feel about themselves, ultimately leading to increased self-confidence.

Comparison to others: Comparing oneself to others can be a significant obstacle to building self-confidence. Social media and other platforms often make it easy to compare oneself to others, which can lead to feelings of inadequacy and self-doubt. To overcome this obstacle, individuals need to recognize that everyone has their unique strengths and weaknesses and that comparing oneself to others is an unproductive and unnecessary exercise. Instead, individuals should focus on their personal growth and development, celebrating their successes and learning from their failures.

Lack of support: Building self-confidence can be challenging, and having a supportive network of friends, family, or a therapist can be incredibly helpful. Lack of support can make individuals feel isolated and alone, making it harder to build self-confidence. To overcome this obstacle, individuals can seek out supportive communities or individuals who share similar goals and values. They can also consider working with a therapist or coach to help them overcome their self-doubt and build self-confidence.

Past Trauma: Past traumatic experiences can impact self-confidence, making it challenging to build trust in oneself and others. Trauma can lead to feelings of shame, guilt, and self-doubt, hindering an individual's ability to build self-confidence. To overcome this obstacle, individuals may need to seek professional help from a therapist or trauma specialist to address and heal from past traumas. With the right support and guidance, individuals can learn to rebuild their sense of self and develop healthy self-confidence.

Overall, building self-confidence is a journey that requires dedication, patience, and resilience. By recognizing and addressing obstacles, individuals can overcome their self-doubt and develop the self-confidence they need to live fulfilling and meaningful lives.

CHAPTER FOUR

LEARNING FROM FAILURE

A. Overcoming fear of failure

Overcoming fear of failure is an important step in building self-confidence. Fear of failure is a common phenomenon and it is something that everyone experiences at some point in their life. This fear can be so strong that it stops people from taking risks, trying new things, or pursuing their goals. However, it is important to remember that failure is a normal part of life and that everyone fails at some point.

One of the main reasons people fear failure is because they are afraid of the consequences of failing. They might worry that they will be judged or criticized by others, or that they will lose their job or suffer other negative consequences. However, it is important to recognize that the consequences of failure are often not as bad as they seem. In fact, many successful people have experienced failure before they achieved their goals.

To overcome fear of failure, it is important to develop a growth mindset. This means recognizing that failure is an opportunity to learn and grow, rather than a sign of inadequacy. When you have a growth mindset, you are more likely to take risks and try new things, even if there is a risk of failure.

Another important way to overcome fear of failure is to reframe the way you think about failure. Instead of seeing failure as a negative outcome, try to see it as a stepping stone on the path to success. When you fail, take the time to reflect on what you can learn from the experience and how you can use that knowledge to do better next time.

One practical technique for overcoming fear of failure is to set small goals and build on your successes. By achieving small goals, you can build your confidence and gradually work your way up to bigger goals. This will help you develop a sense of accomplishment and increase your motivation to pursue bigger goals.

Another effective technique is to use positive self-talk. When you catch yourself thinking negative thoughts about failure, try to reframe those thoughts in a more positive way. For example, instead of thinking "I‘m going to fail," try thinking "I’m going to do my best and learn from whatever happens."

Overall, overcoming fear of failure is an important step in building self-confidence. By developing a growth mindset, reframing the way you think about failure, setting small goals, and using positive self-talk, you can build your confidence and achieve your goals.

B. Reframing failures as learning opportunities

One of the biggest obstacles to building self-confidence is the fear of failure. Many people avoid taking risks or trying new things because they are afraid of failing or making mistakes. However, this fear can be overcome by reframing failures as learning opportunities.

Instead of seeing failure as a negative outcome, it can be viewed as a necessary step towards success. Thomas Edison, inventor of the light bulb, famously said, “I have not failed. I’ve just found 10,000 ways that won’t work.” Edison understood that failure is a necessary part of the process of innovation and that it provides valuable feedback for future efforts.

To reframe failures as learning opportunities, it is important to shift one's mindset from a fixed mindset to a growth mindset. A fixed mindset sees failure as evidence of one's limitations, whereas a growth mindset sees failure as an opportunity for growth and development.

Practical techniques for reframing failures as learning opportunities include:

Reframing the language around failure: Instead of saying "I failed," try saying "I learned" or "I discovered." This shift in language can help to change one's mindset and see failure in a more positive light.

Journaling: Writing about one's experiences with failure can help to process the emotions and learn from the experience. Journaling can also be a way to track progress over time and celebrate small wins along the way.

Mindfulness: Practicing mindfulness can help to reduce the impact of negative thoughts and emotions associated with failure. By focusing on the present moment and accepting one's thoughts and feelings without judgment, one can develop a more positive and resilient mindset.

Seeking feedback: Asking for feedback from others can provide valuable insights and help to identify areas for improvement. This feedback can be used to make adjustments and approach future challenges with a more informed and confident mindset.

Real-life examples of reframing failures as learning opportunities include:

The story of Michael Jordan: Michael Jordan is one of the greatest basketball players of all time, but he did not achieve success without experiencing failure. Jordan was cut from his high school basketball team, but instead of giving up, he used this failure as motivation to work harder and improve his skills. Jordan later said, "I've missed more than 9000 shots in my career. I've lost almost 300 games. 26 times, I've been trusted to take the game-winning shot and missed. I've failed over and over and over again in my life. And that is why I succeed."

The story of J.K. Rowling: J.K. Rowling, author of the Harry Potter series, faced many rejections from publishers before finally getting her first book published. She has said that these rejections were a valuable learning experience and helped her to develop a thicker skin and persevere in the face of adversity. Rowling has also said, "It is impossible to live without failing at something, unless you live so cautiously that you might as well not have lived at all – in which case, you fail by default."

By reframing failures as learning opportunities and approaching challenges with a growth mindset, individuals can develop greater resilience and self-confidence.

C. Using past failures to motivate and inspire personal growth

Using past failures to motivate and inspire personal growth is an effective way to overcome self-doubt and build self-confidence. When we view failures as opportunities to learn and grow, we shift our focus from the negative experience to the positive outcome. Here are some ways to use past failures to inspire personal growth:

Reflect on the lessons learned: When we experience failure, it's important to take time to reflect on what went wrong and what we can learn from the experience. By doing this, we can gain valuable insights into our strengths and weaknesses, as well as develop a plan for moving forward.

Set new goals: After reflecting on our past failures, it's important to set new goals that are realistic and achievable. By setting new goals, we can take what we have learned and apply it to our future endeavors.

Use failure as motivation: Failure can be a powerful motivator if we allow it to be. By using our past failures as motivation, we can push ourselves to work harder and achieve more than we ever thought possible.

Share your story: Sharing our stories of failure and how we overcame them can inspire others to do the same. By being vulnerable and open about our failures, we can create a sense of community and support for others who may be struggling with self-doubt.

Practice self-compassion: It's important to be kind and compassionate to ourselves when we experience failure. By practicing self-compassion, we can learn to accept ourselves for who we are, failures and all.

In conclusion, using past failures to motivate and inspire personal growth is a powerful way to overcome self-doubt and build self-confidence. By reflecting on our failures, setting new goals, using failure as motivation, sharing our stories, and practicing self-compassion, we can transform our failures into opportunities for growth and development.

CHAPTER FIVE

Embracing Vulnerability

A. The benefits of vulnerability

Vulnerability is often thought of as a weakness, but it is actually a source of strength that can help us build deeper connections with others, develop emotional resilience, and foster personal growth. In this section, we will explore the benefits of vulnerability in more detail.

One of the key benefits of vulnerability is that it allows us to be more authentic. When we are vulnerable, we are being honest and open about our emotions, thoughts, and experiences. This authenticity can help us build deeper connections with others because people are drawn to those who are genuine and real. By being vulnerable, we are showing our true selves, which can help others relate to us and form stronger bonds.

Another benefit of vulnerability is that it helps us develop emotional resilience. When we allow ourselves to be vulnerable, we are exposing ourselves to the possibility of rejection or failure. This can be scary, but it can also help us build emotional strength and resilience. By facing our fears and insecurities, we become better equipped to handle difficult situations in the future. We learn that we can survive and even thrive in the face of adversity, which can be a powerful source of strength and confidence.

Vulnerability also takes courage. It takes bravery to face our fears and expose ourselves to the possibility of rejection or failure. By practicing vulnerability, we can develop a sense of courage that we can apply to other areas of our lives. This can help us take risks and try new things, which can be essential for personal growth and development.

In addition to building courage and resilience, vulnerability can also help us develop self-awareness. When we allow ourselves to be vulnerable, we gain a better understanding of our own emotions, motivations, and values. This self-awareness can help us make better decisions and lead a more fulfilling life. By understanding our own needs and desires, we can make choices that are more aligned with our true selves.

Finally, vulnerability can be a source of creativity. When we allow ourselves to take risks and try new things, we open ourselves up to new ideas and possibilities. This can help us break out of old patterns and think more creatively about our lives and the world around us.

In conclusion, vulnerability is not a weakness, but a strength. By being vulnerable, we can build deeper connections with others, develop emotional resilience, foster personal growth, and tap into our creativity. While vulnerability can be scary, it can also be a powerful source of strength and confidence. By embracing vulnerability, we can live more authentic, fulfilling lives.

B. Strategies for becoming more comfortable with vulnerability

While vulnerability can lead to increased connections and personal growth, it can also be uncomfortable and difficult to embrace. However, with practice and intentionality, it is possible to become more comfortable with vulnerability. Below are some strategies to help in this process:

Acknowledge and accept your vulnerabilities: Recognizing and accepting your own vulnerabilities is an important first step in becoming more comfortable with vulnerability. Acknowledge the emotions you feel and allow yourself to experience them without judgment.

Practice self-compassion: Self-compassion involves treating yourself with kindness, care, and concern when things don't go as planned or when you experience difficult emotions. This helps to create a safe and supportive environment for yourself, which can make it easier to be vulnerable.

Challenge negative beliefs and thoughts: Negative beliefs and thoughts can hold us back from being vulnerable. Challenging these beliefs and thoughts can help to create a more positive mindset and make it easier to embrace vulnerability.

Start small: It's important not to overwhelm yourself with vulnerability. Start small by being vulnerable with someone you trust, such as a close friend or family member. As you become more comfortable, you can gradually increase the level of vulnerability.

Set boundaries: While vulnerability can be empowering, it's important to set boundaries and be mindful of who you share your vulnerabilities with. It's important to trust the person you are sharing with and to make sure that you are emotionally safe.

Practice active listening: Being an active listener and showing empathy towards others can help to create a safe space for vulnerability. This can lead to deeper connections and trust with others, making it easier to be vulnerable in return.

Real example: Imagine you have been struggling with anxiety for years, but have always kept it hidden from those around you. You start to open up to a close friend about your struggles and find that they are incredibly supportive and understanding. Over time, you begin to share more and more about your anxiety, and in doing so, you find that your anxiety starts to feel less overwhelming. By being vulnerable, you were able to create a deeper connection with your friend and make progress in managing your anxiety.

C. How vulnerability can lead to more authentic relationships

When we are vulnerable, we allow ourselves to be seen and known for who we truly are, which can create deeper connections with others. Here are some ways in which vulnerability can lead to more authentic relationships:

Trust: When we are vulnerable with someone, we are showing them that we trust them enough to share our true selves. This can create a sense of trust in the relationship, as the other person knows that we are being open and honest with them.

Connection: Vulnerability can create a sense of connection between people, as we are sharing something meaningful and personal with another person. This can lead to a deeper understanding and appreciation of each other.

Empathy: When we are vulnerable with others, we give them the opportunity to empathize with us and our struggles. This can lead to a greater sense of compassion and understanding in the relationship.

Acceptance: By showing our vulnerabilities, we give others permission to do the same. This can create an environment of acceptance, where people feel safe to be themselves without fear of judgment.

Growth: Vulnerability can also lead to personal growth, as we confront our fears and insecurities and work through them with the help of others. This can lead to a stronger sense of self and a more positive outlook on life.

So, how can we become more comfortable with vulnerability and reap the benefits of more authentic relationships? Here are some strategies:

Practice self-compassion: Being vulnerable can be scary, so it's important to be kind and gentle with ourselves when we are taking these risks. Practice self-compassion by speaking to yourself in a kind and supportive way, just as you would speak to a good friend.

Start small: Vulnerability doesn't have to be a big, dramatic reveal. Start by sharing something small and personal with someone you trust, and see how it feels. Over time, you can work up to sharing more significant parts of yourself.

Choose your audience wisely: While vulnerability can be a strength, it's important to be mindful of who you share your vulnerabilities with. Choose people who are trustworthy, supportive, and non-judgmental.

Be present: When we are vulnerable, we are often revealing parts of ourselves that we may have kept hidden. It's important to be present and engaged in the moment, rather than letting our minds wander to what the other person might be thinking.

Embrace discomfort: Vulnerability can be uncomfortable, but it's important to embrace that discomfort and push through it. Remember that growth and connection often come from taking risks and stepping outside our comfort zone.

By becoming more comfortable with vulnerability, we can create more authentic and fulfilling relationships with those around us. It takes practice and courage, but the rewards are well worth it.

CHAPTER SIX

Cultivating a Growth Mindset

A. Definition and benefits of a growth mindset

A growth mindset is a mindset that believes that abilities and qualities can be developed through dedication and hard work. In contrast to a fixed mindset, which believes that abilities and qualities are largely predetermined and unchangeable, a growth mindset sees setbacks and challenges as opportunities for growth and learning. The benefits of having a growth mindset are numerous, and research has shown that cultivating a growth mindset can lead to greater success, resilience, and well-being.

One of the key benefits of a growth mindset is increased motivation. People with a growth mindset are more likely to be intrinsically motivated, meaning that they are motivated by the process of learning and improving rather than external rewards or pressures. This motivation can be particularly helpful in challenging or difficult situations, as it encourages individuals to persist and work through obstacles rather than giving up or becoming discouraged.

Another benefit of a growth mindset is greater resilience. People with a growth mindset are better equipped to handle setbacks and failures because they view them as opportunities for learning and growth. This can lead to greater perseverance, as well as increased creativity and innovation.

A growth mindset can also lead to greater well-being. When individuals believe that they can develop and improve their abilities and qualities, they are more likely to engage in self-care behaviors and prioritize their mental and physical health. Additionally, a growth mindset can lead to greater self-esteem and self-confidence, as individuals recognize their ability to overcome challenges and achieve their goals.

Overall, a growth mindset can be a powerful tool for personal growth and development. By recognizing the potential for growth and learning in every situation, individuals can become more motivated, resilient, and self-assured.

B. Techniques for developing a growth mindset, such as mindfulness, positive self-talk, and self-reflection

Developing a growth mindset is not a one-time achievement but rather a continuous journey of self-improvement. However, certain techniques can help individuals develop a growth mindset more effectively. Here are some techniques that can be helpful:

Practice mindfulness: Mindfulness involves being present in the moment without judgment. It can help individuals become more aware of their thoughts and emotions, which is an essential step in developing a growth mindset. By becoming more mindful, individuals can recognize when they are having a fixed mindset and choose to shift to a growth mindset. Mindfulness can be practiced through meditation, breathing exercises, or simply paying attention to the present moment.

Use positive self-talk: Positive self-talk involves consciously choosing to focus on positive thoughts and beliefs about oneself. This technique can help individuals develop a growth mindset by encouraging them to believe that their abilities and skills are not fixed but can be developed through effort and learning. Positive self-talk can involve affirmations, visualizations, or simply replacing negative self-talk with more positive and encouraging statements.

Engage in self-reflection: Self-reflection involves taking time to think about one's experiences, emotions, and beliefs. By reflecting on past experiences, individuals can identify patterns of thought and behavior that may be limiting their growth. Self-reflection can help individuals challenge their fixed mindset beliefs and develop more growth-oriented beliefs.

Embrace challenges: Embracing challenges is an important part of developing a growth mindset. When faced with a challenge, individuals with a growth mindset see it as an opportunity to learn and grow. They are not afraid to fail because they understand that failure is a natural part of the learning process. Embracing challenges can involve taking on new tasks, learning new skills, or pushing oneself out of their comfort zone.

Seek feedback: Seeking feedback is an important part of developing a growth mindset. Feedback can provide valuable information about one's strengths and weaknesses and help individuals identify areas for improvement. Individuals with a growth mindset are not afraid to receive feedback because they understand that it can help them grow and improve.

By practicing these techniques, individuals can develop a growth mindset and begin to approach life with a more open and optimistic attitude. This can lead to greater personal and professional success, as well as a greater sense of fulfillment and happiness.

C. Overcoming fixed mindset thinking patterns

While developing a growth mindset is essential to personal growth, it is equally important to recognize and address fixed mindset thinking patterns that can impede progress. Fixed mindset thinking involves the belief that one's abilities and traits are set in stone and cannot be changed. This kind of thinking can lead to fear of failure, resistance to challenges, and a lack of willingness to learn and improve. However, with deliberate effort and the right strategies, it is possible to overcome these fixed mindset thinking patterns and cultivate a more open and adaptable mindset.

Here are some techniques for overcoming fixed mindset thinking patterns:

Recognize and challenge negative self-talk: Fixed mindset thinking often involves self-defeating and limiting beliefs. These beliefs can become internalized and self-reinforcing, making it difficult to break out of negative patterns. However, by paying attention to our self-talk and challenging negative thoughts, we can begin to shift our mindset towards growth. When a negative thought arises, ask yourself whether it is based on evidence or simply a self-imposed limitation.

Embrace challenges: Fixed mindset thinking can make us resistant to challenges and new experiences. However, challenges are a necessary part of growth and learning. By embracing challenges, we can develop new skills and overcome our limitations. Start small and gradually work up to bigger challenges, using each experience as an opportunity for growth and learning.

Focus on the process, not just the outcome: Fixed mindset thinking often centers around the belief that success or failure is predetermined by our innate abilities. However, by shifting our focus to the process of learning and growth, we can cultivate a more open and adaptable mindset. Rather than worrying about whether we will succeed or fail, we can focus on the steps we are taking to improve and grow.

Practice self-compassion: Fixed mindset thinking can lead to self-criticism and a lack of self-compassion. However, self-compassion is essential for personal growth and development. By practicing self-compassion, we can learn to accept and learn from our mistakes, rather than letting them define us.

Seek feedback: Fixed mindset thinking can make us resistant to feedback, as we may fear that it will confirm our limitations. However, feedback is essential for growth and development. Seek out constructive feedback from trusted sources and use it as an opportunity to learn and improve.

In conclusion, fixed mindset thinking patterns can be a significant barrier to personal growth and development. However, by recognizing these patterns and using the right strategies, we can cultivate a more open and adaptable mindset, embrace challenges, and achieve our full potential.

CHAPTER SEVEN

Seeking Support

A. The importance of support for overcoming self-doubt

Support can be a critical factor in overcoming self-doubt. It is essential to have a strong support system in place to help navigate the difficulties that come with challenging negative beliefs and building self-confidence. Having a support system can make a significant difference in both the short and long term.

One of the most significant benefits of having a support system is the sense of belonging and validation that it provides. When someone experiences self-doubt, they may feel isolated and alone in their struggles. Having a supportive friend or family member who is willing to listen and offer encouragement can help alleviate these feelings and provide a sense of connection.

Moreover, a supportive network can provide valuable feedback and insight. Sometimes, when an individual experiences self-doubt, their thoughts may become distorted, making it difficult to see the situation clearly. Friends or family members can provide an objective perspective and help them identify negative self-talk and patterns of thinking that are holding them back.

Support can come from various sources, including family members, friends, coaches, mentors, or therapists. Each of these individuals can provide different forms of support, depending on their relationship with the individual and their expertise. For instance, a therapist can offer professional support and help an individual develop specific coping strategies to manage their self-doubt. A coach or mentor can offer guidance and encouragement in a particular area of interest or goal.

It is essential to communicate clearly with your support system about your needs and how they can help. Sometimes, it can be challenging to ask for help, but being open and honest about what you need can help ensure that you receive the support you require. For example, if you need someone to help hold you accountable for specific goals or tasks, communicating this to a supportive friend or mentor can help you stay on track.

Finally, it is vital to remember that self-doubt is a common experience, and there is no shame in seeking support. Many people struggle with self-doubt, and having a supportive network in place can help individuals feel less alone in their struggles. Moreover, the support and encouragement of others can provide the motivation and inspiration necessary to overcome self-doubt and achieve personal goals.

In conclusion, having a strong support system can play a vital role in overcoming self-doubt. It provides a sense of belonging, validation, and perspective, helping individuals navigate their struggles and achieve their goals. Whether it comes from family members, friends, coaches, mentors, or therapists, support is a critical component of personal growth and development.

B. How to identify and build a supportive network

Having a strong support system is essential when it comes to overcoming self-doubt. This support system can include family, friends, mentors, and peers who provide encouragement, guidance, and a listening ear. In this section, we'll explore how to identify and build a supportive network.

Identify potential sources of support: The first step is to identify potential sources of support. This could include family members, friends, colleagues, mentors, or even online communities. Think about the people in your life who have been supportive in the past and who you feel comfortable sharing your struggles with.

Reach out and ask for support: Once you've identified potential sources of support, it's important to reach out and ask for help. This can be a difficult step, especially if you're used to keeping your struggles to yourself. But remember, people who care about you want to help you and see you succeed.

Be specific about your needs: When you ask for support, be specific about your needs. Let your support system know what you're struggling with and how they can best help you. For example, if you're feeling overwhelmed with work, you might ask a colleague to help you prioritize your tasks.

Build a diverse support network: It's important to build a diverse support network that includes people with different backgrounds, perspectives, and areas of expertise. This can provide a well-rounded approach to problem-solving and support.

Be willing to reciprocate: Building a supportive network is a two-way street. While it's important to ask for help when you need it, it's also important to be willing to reciprocate when others need support. This can help build stronger relationships and a more supportive community.

Nurture your support system: Finally, it's important to nurture your support system. This means staying in touch with the people who have supported you, showing your appreciation, and being there for them when they need it.

In conclusion, building a supportive network is an important step in overcoming self-doubt. It can provide encouragement, guidance, and a listening ear, which can help you to stay motivated and focused on your goals. Remember to be specific about your needs, build a diverse support network, and be willing to reciprocate. And don't forget to show your appreciation and nurture your relationships with your support system.

C. The role of mentors, friends, family, and professionals in supporting personal development

Having a supportive network is crucial in overcoming self-doubt and building self-confidence. Support can come from a variety of sources, including mentors, friends, family, and professionals.

Mentors can provide guidance, advice, and support as you work towards your personal and professional goals. They can offer insights from their own experiences, and help you to see your own potential. For example, a mentor might help you to identify and develop your strengths, or provide you with feedback and encouragement as you work towards a new goal.

Friends and family can also play a vital role in supporting personal development. They can offer emotional support, a listening ear, and a sense of community. Surrounding yourself with positive, encouraging people can help to counteract the negative self-talk that often accompanies self-doubt. For example, a friend might help you to see the progress you've made towards a goal, or provide encouragement when you're feeling discouraged.

Professionals can also be a valuable source of support in overcoming self-doubt. This might include therapists, coaches, or other mental health professionals. These professionals can help you to identify and address the underlying causes of your self-doubt, and provide you with tools and strategies for building self-confidence. For example, a therapist might help you to identify and challenge negative thought patterns, or provide you with mindfulness exercises to help you stay present and focused.

Real-life examples of the power of support in overcoming self-doubt are abundant. For instance, a person struggling with self-doubt about their ability to launch a new business might find guidance and support from a mentor who has already achieved success in their field. Alternatively, a person dealing with self-doubt related to a traumatic experience might benefit from the emotional support of a friend or family member who can listen and empathize with their struggles. Similarly, a person dealing with anxiety or depression might find relief through the professional support of a therapist or mental health professional.

In short, building a supportive network is an essential part of overcoming self-doubt and building self-confidence. Whether it's through the guidance of a mentor, the emotional support of friends and family, or the professional assistance of a therapist, the power of support should not be underestimated.

CHAPTER EIGHT

TAKING ACTION

A. Setting and achieving goals

Setting and achieving goals is an important aspect of personal development, and it can help individuals overcome self-doubt by providing a sense of purpose, direction, and accomplishment. Goals can be short-term or long-term, and they can be related to personal or professional areas of life. Here are some details on how to set and achieve goals to overcome self-doubt:

Defining your goals is an important step in achieving success and overcoming self-doubt. When you set clear, specific, and achievable goals, you give yourself something to work towards and a sense of direction. This can help you stay motivated and focused, and provide a sense of accomplishment as you make progress towards achieving your goals.

To define your goals, start by thinking about what you want to achieve. Consider both short-term and long-term goals, and make sure they are realistic and achievable. It can be helpful to break your goals down into smaller, more manageable steps, as this can make them feel less overwhelming.

Once you have identified your goals, it can be helpful to write them down and create a plan for achieving them. This plan should include specific actions you will take to move closer to your goals, as well as a timeline for when you hope to achieve them. It can also be helpful to track your progress along the way, as this can help you stay motivated and make adjustments as needed.

For example, if your goal is to start a new business, you might break that goal down into smaller steps such as researching your market, creating a business plan, finding funding, and launching your product or service. By breaking your goal down into smaller steps, you can work on them one at a time, and track your progress as you go.

Defining your goals can help you overcome self-doubt by providing a clear focus and a sense of purpose. When you have a clear idea of what you want to achieve, you can work towards that goal with confidence and determination, rather than feeling overwhelmed and uncertain about what to do next.

A. Create a plan:
Once you have identified your goals, it's important to create a plan that outlines the steps you will take to achieve them. This plan should be specific, measurable, achievable, relevant, and time-bound. Consider breaking your goal down into smaller, more manageable tasks to help you stay on track and feel a sense of progress. Your plan should also include potential obstacles and strategies for overcoming them.

B. Stay focused:
Staying focused on your goals can be a challenge, especially when life gets busy or setbacks occur. To help stay focused, try visualizing the end result of achieving your goal and the positive impact it will have on your life. You may also want to enlist the support of a friend, family member, or mentor who can help keep you accountable and motivated.

C. Learn from setbacks:
Setbacks and failures are a natural part of the goal-setting process, but it's important to use these experiences as opportunities for learning and growth. Take some time to reflect on what went wrong and what you could have done differently. Use this information to adjust your plan and move forward in a more informed and

confident way.

Real-life example:

Let's say your goal is to run a 5k race in three months. Your plan might include running three times a week, gradually increasing your mileage, and incorporating strength training exercises to prevent injury. To stay focused, you might visualize yourself crossing the finish line, feeling strong and accomplished. You might also enlist a friend to join you for your runs or check in with you regularly to see how your training is going. If you experience a setback, such as an injury or a missed training session, you might reflect on what led to the setback and adjust your plan accordingly, perhaps by incorporating more rest days or seeking advice from a professional. By learning from setbacks and staying focused on your plan, you can increase your chances of achieving your goal.

B. The power of small steps and incremental progress

The power of small steps and incremental progress is a concept that has been around for a long time, and it has been embraced by many successful people in various fields. It is a simple idea that involves breaking down larger goals into smaller, more manageable tasks and focusing on making progress, no matter how small. In this article, we will explore the benefits of small steps and incremental progress, and how you can apply this concept in your own life.

One of the key benefits of taking small steps and making incremental progress is that it can help to reduce the feeling of overwhelm. When we set big goals for ourselves, it can be easy to become discouraged by the magnitude of the task at hand. However, when we break those goals down into smaller, more manageable steps, we can begin to see progress and build momentum.

Another benefit of small steps and incremental progress is that it can help to build confidence. When we see that we are making progress, no matter how small, it can give us a sense of accomplishment and help to reinforce the belief that we are capable of achieving our goals. This can be especially important when we are facing challenges or setbacks.

Making small steps and incremental progress can also help to create momentum. When we focus on making progress, even if it's just a little bit each day, we can start to build momentum towards our goals. This momentum can be self-reinforcing, as we begin to see the positive effects of our efforts and become more motivated to continue.

So how can you apply the concept of small steps and incremental progress in your own life? One way is to break down your larger goals into smaller, more manageable tasks. For example, if your goal is to write a book, you might start by setting a goal to write for 15 minutes a day, or to write 100 words a day. These small steps may not seem like much, but over time they can add up to significant progress.

Another way to make small steps and incremental progress is to track your progress. This can be as simple as keeping a journal or spreadsheet of the tasks you complete each day. Seeing your progress in black and white can be a powerful motivator and can help to keep you on track.

Finally, it's important to remember that small steps and incremental progress are not a quick fix. They require patience, persistence, and consistency. But by focusing on making progress, no matter how small, you can begin to build momentum towards your goals and create positive change in your life.

In conclusion, the power of small steps and incremental progress is a simple yet powerful concept that can help you to achieve your goals and live a more fulfilling life. By breaking down larger goals into smaller, more manageable tasks, focusing on progress, and tracking your progress, you can build momentum towards your goals and achieve success. So take that first small step today, and watch as your progress begins to add up over time.

C. The role of action in building confidence and overcoming self-doubt

Action plays a critical role in building confidence and overcoming self-doubt. Self-doubt can be paralyzing, making it difficult to take action and pursue our goals. However, taking action, even in small steps, can help to break this cycle of self-doubt and build confidence.

Here are some ways that action can help to build confidence and overcome self-doubt:

Proving to yourself that you are capable: When we take action, even in small steps, we prove to ourselves that we are capable of achieving our goals. This can help to build confidence and self-belief.

Breaking the cycle of self-doubt: Self-doubt can be a vicious cycle. The more we doubt ourselves, the less likely we are to take action. Taking action can help to break this cycle and build momentum towards our goals.

Learning and growing: When we take action, we have the opportunity to learn and grow from our experiences. This can help to build our skills and knowledge, as well as our confidence.

Building resilience: Taking action also helps to build resilience, which is the ability to bounce back from setbacks and challenges. Building resilience can help us to overcome self-doubt and build confidence in our ability to handle whatever comes our way.

To take action and build confidence, start with small steps. Identify one action that you can take today, no matter how small, that will move you closer to your goals. Celebrate your progress and use it as a source of motivation to continue taking action. Remember, every action you take, no matter how small, is a step towards building confidence and overcoming self-doubt.

CHAPTER NINE

CONCLUSION

Recap of key points

To recap, here are the key points about the role of action in building confidence and overcoming self-doubt:

Taking action can help to prove to yourself that you are capable of achieving your goals, which can build confidence and self-belief.

When we take action, we break the cycle of self-doubt and build momentum towards our goals.

Taking action also provides opportunities to learn and grow, which can increase our skills and knowledge, as well as our confidence.

Building resilience through taking action helps us to bounce back from setbacks and challenges, which can help us to overcome self-doubt and build confidence in our ability to handle difficult situations.

Starting with small steps and celebrating progress can be a powerful motivator to continue taking action towards our goals.

Overall, taking action is an essential part of building confidence and overcoming self-doubt. By taking small steps towards our goals and celebrating our progress, we can break the cycle of self-doubt and build momentum towards a more confident and fulfilling life.

CHAPTER TEN

ENCOURAGEMENT AND INSPIRATION

If you're reading this, chances are you have experienced self-doubt at some point in your life. It can be a challenging and isolating experience, but I want to encourage you to keep going and never give up.

Remember that everyone experiences self-doubt at some point in their lives. It's a natural and normal part of the human experience. The good news is that self-doubt doesn't have to control your life. With the right tools and strategies, you can learn to overcome it and build confidence in yourself.

One of the most important things you can do is to take action, no matter how small. Every step you take towards your goals, no matter how small, is a step towards building confidence and overcoming self-doubt. Celebrate your progress and use it as a source of motivation to keep going.

Another important strategy is to reframe your thoughts. When you notice negative self-talk, challenge it with positive and affirming statements. Surround yourself with positive and supportive people who believe in you and your goals.

Lastly, remember to be kind and compassionate to yourself. Self-doubt can be a painful and challenging experience, but it doesn't have to define you. Take care of yourself and prioritize self-care, which can help to reduce stress and increase confidence.

You have the power to overcome self-doubt and build the confidence to pursue your dreams. With the right mindset and strategies, you can rise above self-doubt and achieve your full potential. Remember, you are capable of great things, and you deserve to believe in yourself.

Printed by Libri Plureos GmbH in Hamburg,
Germany